The Nile

River in the Sand

By Molly Aloian

CRABTREE
Publishing Company
www.crabtreebooks.com

Crabtree Publishing Company
www.crabtreebooks.com

Author: Molly Aloian
Editor: Barbara Bakowski
Designer: Tammy West, Westgraphix LLC
Photo Researcher: Edward A. Thomas
Map Illustrator: Stefan Chabluk
Indexer: Nila Glikin
Project Coordinator: Kathy Middleton
Crabtree Editor: Adrianna Morganelli
Production Coordinator: Kenneth Wright
Prepress Technician: Kenneth Wright

Series Consultant: Michael E. Ritter, Ph.D., Professor of Geography, University of Wisconsin—Stevens Point

Developed for Crabtree Publishing Company by RJF Publishing LLC (www.RJFpublishing.com)

Photo Credits:
Cover: AP Images;
4, 7, 10, 11, 16, 18, 20, 23, 24, 27: iStockphoto
6: Imagine Images/Alastair Pidgen/Shutterstock
8: © Danita Delimont/Alamy
12: Simon Grosset/Imagestate RM/Photolibrary
14: Radius Images/Photolibrary
19: AFP/Getty Images
22: © Jon Arnold Images Ltd./Alamy
25: © Tony Roddam/Alamy

Cover: Traditional boats called feluccas sail on the Nile River near the pyramids at Giza in Egypt.

Library and Archives Canada Cataloguing in Publication

Aloian, Molly
     The Nile : river in the sand / Molly Aloian.

(Rivers around the world)
Includes index.
ISBN 978-0-7787-7445-7 (bound).--ISBN 978-0-7787-7468-6 (pbk.)

     1. Nile River--Juvenile literature. 2. Nile River Valley--Juvenile literature. I. Title. II. Series: Rivers around the world

DT115.A46 2010   j962   C2009-906240-2

Library of Congress Cataloging-in-Publication Data

Aloian, Molly.
 The Nile : river in the sand / by Molly Aloian.
     p. cm. -- (Rivers around the world)
 Includes index.
 ISBN 978-0-7787-7468-6 (pbk. : alk. paper)–ISBN 978-0-7787-7445-7 (reinforced library binding : alk. paper)
 1. Nile River--Juvenile literature. 2. Nile River Valley--Juvenile literature. I. Title. II. Series.

DT115.A46 2009
962--dc22
                                        2009042407

Crabtree Publishing Company
www.crabtreebooks.com   1-800-387-7650

Printed in the U.S.A./122009/BG20091103

Published in Canada
Crabtree Publishing
616 Welland Ave.
St. Catharines, ON
L2M 5V6

Published in the United States
Crabtree Publishing
PMB 59051
350 Fifth Avenue, 59th Floor
New York, New York 10118

Published in the United Kingdom
Crabtree Publishing
Maritime House
Basin Road North, Hove
BN41 1WR

Published in Australia
Crabtree Publishing
386 Mt. Alexander Rd.
Ascot Vale (Melbourne)
VIC 3032

CONTENTS

Words that are defined in the glossary are in **bold** type
the first time they appear in the text.

CHAPTER 1

The River in the Sand

The Nile River is the world's longest waterway. It starts in east-central Africa and flows north for 4,145 miles (6,670 kilometers). The river flows through farmland, swamps, large cities, and small villages. The Nile also crosses the Sahara, the world's largest hot desert. Ancient Egyptians called the Nile "the river in the sand" because water seemed to mysteriously arise from the dry sands of the Sahara. Few plants and animals can survive in the Sahara, except along the banks of the Nile.

FAST FACT

The White Nile gets its name from the color of clay in its waters. The Blue Nile sometimes looks black, and the word for black and blue is the same in the local Sudanese dialect.

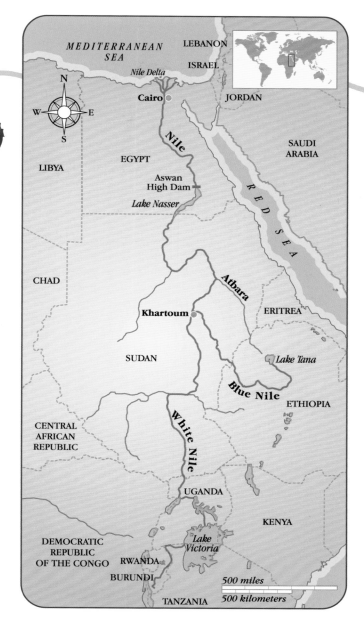

Beginning in east-central Africa, the Nile River flows north for about 4,145 miles (6,670 km) to the Mediterranean Sea.

From Source to Sea

The Nile River has a long, complex course. It is formed by two main branches, the White Nile and the Blue Nile, that join at Khartoum, in Sudan. Hundreds of smaller **tributaries** join the Nile River at various points along its course. One of the largest and most important tributaries is the Atbara River, which flows into the Nile River about 200 miles (320 km) north of Khartoum. The river then flows through the arid Sahara. After reaching the city of Cairo, in Egypt, the Nile River divides into several smaller streams, forming a **delta**. At the **mouth** of the Nile River, the water empties into the Mediterranean Sea.

The Life-Giving Nile

Human civilizations have relied on the Nile River for more than 5,000 years. Each summer, the Nile River flooded in Egypt. The ancient Egyptians looked

LEFT: The Philae Temple is really a complex of temples on a small island south of Aswan, Egypt. The main temple is dedicated to the Egyptian goddess Isis.

The Nile River is the main source of water for the millions of people who live along its banks.

forward to the floods because they left nutrient-rich soil for several miles on each side of the river. The fertile soil was good for growing crops. The banks of the Nile became the site of one of the great civilizations of the ancient world. Ancient Egyptians thought the flooding was mysterious and magical. They prayed to the river, praised it in poems, painted pictures of it, and offered sacrifices to it.

The Nile River is still a central part of life and culture for millions of people. People fish in and travel on the Nile River. The river also provides people with drinking water and **irrigation** for crops. **Hydroelectricity** produced by the Nile's flow is a major source of power for the region. Industries rely on water from the Nile River for cleaning and processing many

Running Water

A river is a natural stream of water. Rivers flow in channels and have banks. The water in rivers can come from different sources, including **runoff** and **groundwater**. Some rivers are also fed from melting **glaciers**.

"It was a grand arrangement of Nature for the birth of so mighty and important a stream as the river Nile."

—British explorer Samuel White Baker, in *Ismailia* (1874)

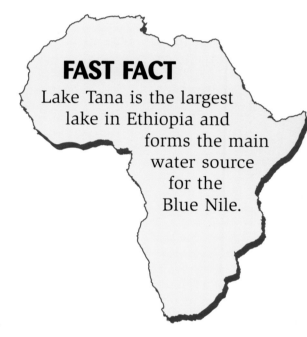

FAST FACT
Lake Tana is the largest lake in Ethiopia and forms the main water source for the Blue Nile.

The Nile hippopotamus lives in a swampy area in the southern part of the Nile River basin. The huge hippo can weigh up to 8,000 pounds (3,630 kg).

products, such as foods and textiles. Tour boats and floating hotels sail the Nile, as well.

Natural World

Thousands of species, or kinds, of plants and animals live in the Nile River and along its banks. Many of these species are **indigenous** to Africa. They help maintain the river's **ecology**. Ecology is the relationship between living and nonliving things and their environment. The plants and animals are also sources of food for millions of people who live in the areas through which the Nile River flows.

CHAPTER 2

The Surface Story

Geologists believe that the Nile River and the land around it did not always look as it does today. These scientists say a system of **rifts** has been pulling parts of the African continent in different directions for millions of years. Rifts are cracks in Earth's crust that widen over time. Rifts created highlands and valleys in eastern Africa. Over time, lakes formed in the valleys and in low spots in the highlands. Water levels rose and spilled over into many streams. As the White Nile began to form, it eventually merged with the Blue Nile at Khartoum. These two waterways created the Nile River that flowed downstream toward the Mediterranean Sea.

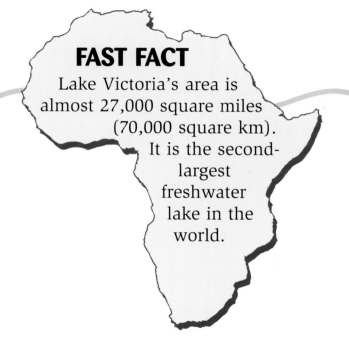

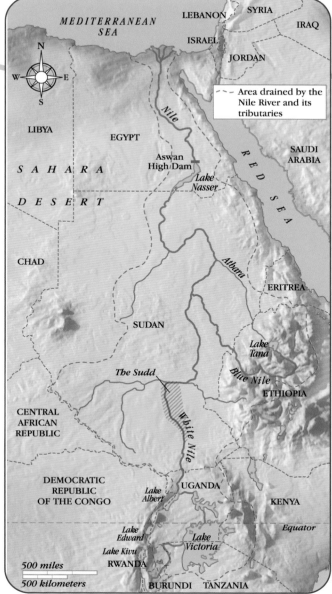

The terrain and the climate vary greatly from the Nile's source in central Africa to the river's mouth at the Mediterranean Sea.

A Source of Mystery

For hundreds of years, explorers and scientists searched for the source of the Nile River. Today, Lake Victoria is generally acknowledged as the river's main source. Lake Victoria, however, has many feeder streams, so some scientists consider the Nile River's most distant source to be a stream that flows out of Nyungwe Forest in southern Rwanda. Some scientists claim, though, that the farthest **headstream** of the Nile River is a small branch of the Kagera River in Burundi.

Nile River Basin

The Nile River and its tributaries drain, or carry away the surface water from, a huge area of land. The area of the **drainage basin** is about 1.3 million square miles (3.3 million square km)—one-tenth the size of the continent of Africa. The Nile River basin includes Egypt, most of Sudan, and parts of Tanzania, Burundi, Rwanda, the Democratic Republic of the Congo, Kenya, Uganda, Ethiopia, and Eritrea.

LEFT: The Tisisat Falls are in northwestern Ethiopia, near Lake Tana, the source of the Blue Nile.

9

Papyrus

Papyrus is one of the Nile River's most important natural resources. Papyrus is a reed-like plant with long stalks. The plants are usually from four to 15 feet (1.2 to 4.6 m) tall! Papyrus helped make learning and education possible for ancient Egyptians. They used the plant to make the earliest form of writing paper. Papyrus paper was both durable and lightweight. People also made boats, ropes, baskets, mats, and other items out of papyrus.

Ancient Egyptians cut papyrus stalks into strips, pressed the strips together, and dried them to form a type of paper.

A **drainage pattern** is the arrangement of a main stream and its tributaries. The drainage pattern is determined by geologic features on and below the surface. The Nile River has a **dendritic** drainage pattern. This pattern develops where an entire basin is made up of the same type of rock. A dendritic drainage pattern looks like the branches of a tree.

Controlling the Flow

Ancient Egyptians celebrated the annual flooding of the Nile River by offering sacrifices and holding processions with the "new water." They never understood what caused the river to overflow. Today, however, people know why the flooding occurred. Heavy rains in the south cause tributaries to swell. Before measures were taken to control the flow, water spilled over the banks and flooded the land for several miles on each side of the river in Egypt.

Today, there are giant dams, canals, and modern irrigation pumps along the Nile River. Dams help control the flow of water and create **reservoirs**. Canals are human-made waterways that are created and used for shipping or irrigation. Because the water level of the Nile River is now controlled, natural flooding no longer occurs in Egypt.

Wild World

Along its course, the Nile River flows through many different regions. It tumbles through rocky mountains, plunges over huge waterfalls, and crosses a hot, dry desert. The river also moves slowly through a swamp called the Sudd. Located in southern

Sudan, the Sudd is the largest swamp in the world.

Thousands of species of plants live in the Nile River and along its banks. Along the Upper Nile—the southern part of the river—there are grasses and trees, such as eucalyptus trees, acacia trees, and oil palm trees. Water hyacinths float in the river. The region surrounding Lake Victoria includes thick tropical forests, low-lying swamps, and grasslands. The Sudd is a hot, wet place with thick plant growth. Farther north, scrub vegetation and short trees grow. Where the Nile River passes through the desert sands of the Sahara, there is very little plant life.

Softshell turtles, monitor lizards, and numerous types of snakes live in and along the Nile River. The northern part of the Nile River flows through the Sahara Desert. The fish that live in the Nile River are some of the few animals that can survive in this dry **habitat**. Fish include the Nile perch, the lungfish, the spiny eel, and many other species. The Nile River is also home to waterbirds such as egrets and herons. In winter, the river attracts millions of **migratory** birds. Birds make nests in the thick vegetation along the Upper Nile's banks. Hundreds of thousands of colorful flamingos gather in shallow areas of the Upper Nile to mate.

The hippopotamus was once common throughout the Nile River basin. As a result of being overhunted, hippos now live only in a swampy area to the south. The Nile crocodile, a fierce **predator** that can be more than 16 feet (five m long) and weigh more than 500 pounds (225 kg), also lives along the Upper Nile.

Crafty Crocodile

The Nile crocodile is a **carnivore**, or meat eater. While hunting, the crocodile keeps its body under water except for the eyeballs and nostrils. The croc creeps close to the riverbank. Then the animal uses its long snout, full of sharp, pointed teeth, to grab a bird, fish, turtle, or other creature that is drinking from the river. A special valve in the crocodile's throat keeps the animal from swallowing water when it opens its mouth under water. The hunter then swallows its meal whole.

A large adult Nile crocodile shows the fearsome teeth that help it catch prey.

People of the Nile

The Nile River—especially its annual flood—was central to the lives of the ancient Egyptians. Each summer, melting snow and heavy rains in central Africa increased the volume of water that entered the Nile River from its tributaries. From June to September, the water in the Nile River rose, and the river in Egypt overflowed its banks. The floodwaters put moisture into the land. They also deposited a layer of rich, dark soil called **silt** alongside the Nile River. The silt contained minerals and other nutrients that helped crops grow well.

The Egyptians planted their crops soon after the floodwaters receded. They grew wheat and vegetables, including beans, peas, cucumbers, and lentils. Vines and fruit trees provided people with grapes, dates, figs, olives, and pomegranates.

Birth of a Civilization

The annual flooding of the Nile River enabled the ancient Egyptians to develop an **economy** based on agriculture. The river also supplied water for drinking and for irrigating crops during the growing season. The ancient Egyptians used a device called a shaduf to draw water from the river for irrigation. The shaduf was made up of a bucket attached to a long pole. Farmers could swing the pole to transfer water from the Nile River into

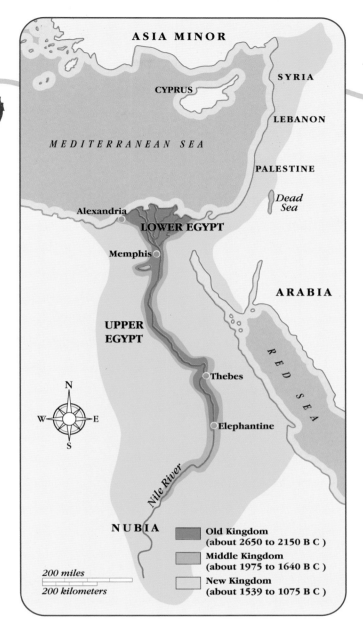

The ancient Egyptian empire grew dramatically over many hundreds of years.

irrigation ditches in their fields. In remote areas, some people still use shadufs today.

People living on the Upper Nile relied on the river for fish. They hunted the birds and land animals that lived along the riverbanks. The river

LEFT: Farm workers grow crops in the fertile soil alongside the Nile River in Luxor, Egypt.

13

Watching the Waters

Ancient Egyptians used special tools to measure the amount of flooding each year. These tools are known today as nilometers. A simple nilometer was a stone pillar with notches marked on it. The notches indicated the rise of the water level during the flood period. Nilometers helped the Egyptians predict the quality of the upcoming harvest. If the flooding was lighter than usual, too little water and nutrients could enter the soil, and crops would not grow as well.

The nilometer on the southern tip of Roda Island in modern Cairo, Egypt, measured the flood levels of the Nile River in ancient times.

was also a source of transportation for people and goods. Ancient Egyptians used wooden barges and sailboats. They also made rafts from papyrus. Because the Nile River provided a plentiful water supply, fertile land for agriculture, and a convenient route for transportation, permanent settlements grew up along the banks of the river.

Pharaohs and Pyramids

The ancient Egyptians built temples overlooking the banks of the Nile River. A temple is a building for worship. The Egyptians also built pyramids as tombs for their kings, called **pharaohs**. A pyramid is a large stone or brick structure that has a rectangular bottom and four sloping, triangular sides that meet.

The ancient Egyptians did not use machines or cranes to build the towering pyramids, statues, palaces, and temples along the Nile River. Hundreds of people worked together using simple tools, including hammers, chisels, and saws. People built ramps of packed earth to move stone blocks. Workers then hauled the blocks up the ramps and put them into place by hand. The Great Pyramid at Giza, built about 4,500 years ago, contains more than two million blocks of stone. Each stone weighs about 2.5 tons (2.3 metric tons). The biggest blocks weigh as much as 14 tons (12.7 metric tons).

Foreign Rule in Egypt

The ancient Egyptian civilization lasted for about 3,000 years before falling to invaders. Persians conquered Egypt in 525 BC. About 200 years later, Greek control of Egypt began when Alexander the Great overthrew the Persian rulers and made Alexandria the capital. In 30 BC, the Roman army attacked Alexandria, ending Greek rule in Egypt and beginning hundreds of years of Roman control.

When the Roman Empire split in the 300s AD, the Eastern Roman Empire, or Byzantine Empire, retained control of Egypt. In 642 AD, Egypt fell to a conquest by armies from what is today Saudi Arabia. The Arabians brought with them the Arabic language and the Islamic faith.

In the 1700s and 1800s, both the French and the British colonized many areas of Africa. France and later Britain effectively controlled Egypt for much of the 1800s and into the 1900s. In 1922, Egypt became an independent country ruled by a king. A republic, or a government made up of elected leaders, was declared in 1953.

NOTABLE QUOTE

"For anyone who sees Egypt, without having heard a word about it before, must perceive, if he has only common powers of observation, that...Egypt...is... the gift of the river."

—ancient Greek historian Herodotus, in *Histories* (440 BC)

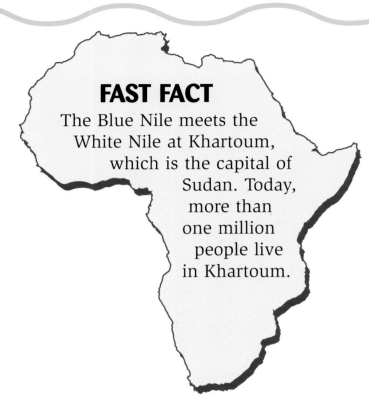

FAST FACT
The Blue Nile meets the White Nile at Khartoum, which is the capital of Sudan. Today, more than one million people live in Khartoum.

Searching for the Source

When the Greek historian Herodotus arrived in Egypt in about 450 BC, he realized the importance of the Nile River to Egypt. However, he could not determine the source of the great river. He wrote: "With regard to the sources of the Nile, I have found no one...who professed to have any knowledge."

A fascination with finding the source of the Nile River endured. In the 1500s and 1600s, European travelers visited Ethiopia, reaching Lake Tana and the source of the Blue Nile in the

Ramses II

Ramses II was one of the longest-ruling pharaohs in Egypt. During his lifetime he gained fame as a warrior, but today he is best known for having built many temples and other structures. There are giant statues of Ramses II throughout Egypt. As recently as 2008, an ancient statue of the pharaoh was discovered beneath the sand in a town on the Nile delta. His **mummy** is preserved in the Egyptian Museum at Cairo.

This statue of Ramses II stands at the temple of Abu Simbel at Aswan, Egypt.

mountains south of the lake. The Spanish priest Pedro Páez wrote an account of Lake Tana in *History of Ethiopia* in 1622. A Scottish explorer, James Bruce, journeyed to Lake Tana in 1770. He reached the headstream of the Blue Nile, which was then thought to be the Nile River's main source.

A British explorer named John Hanning Speke discovered a huge lake while traveling up the White Nile in 1858. The people living in the area called the lake Ukerewe. Speke renamed it Lake Victoria to honor the queen of the United Kingdom. He declared that Lake Victoria was the source of the Nile River.

Livingstone and Stanley

Still, much of Africa remained a mysterious place to people living in Europe. David Livingtone was a

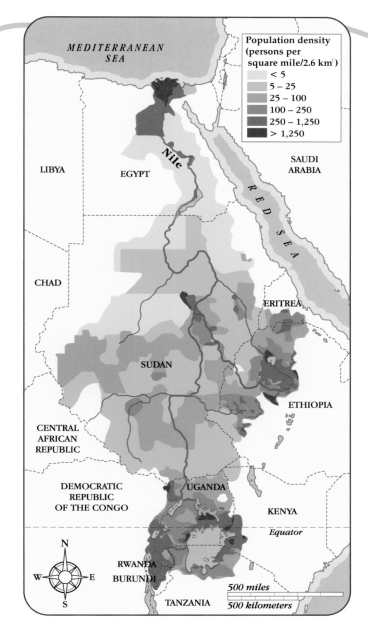

People have long depended on the water of the Nile River. About 95 percent of Egypt's population lives within 12 miles (19 km) of the river.

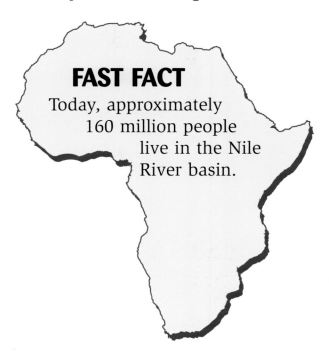

FAST FACT
Today, approximately 160 million people live in the Nile River basin.

Scottish missionary and explorer who traveled throughout Africa. In 1866, he set off on a journey to determine whether Lake Victoria was the true source of the Nile River. For several years after he headed into the interior of the continent, no one heard from Livingstone. A British-born American

Entering the Afterlife

The ancient Egyptians built tombs on the west side of the Nile River. To them, the east stood for rebirth and beginnings, and the west was connected to death. This belief was related to the rising and setting of the Sun. Tombs were located on the west side of the Nile River so that the dead could enter the afterlife.

Ancient burial chambers, like this one at Luxor, were built on the west side of the Nile River.

explorer and newspaper writer, Henry Stanley, was sent to Africa to find Livingstone. In 1871, Stanley discovered Livingstone at Lake Tanganyika, in present-day Tanzania. The two men explored together for a short time before Stanley left Africa. Livingstone continued his search for the source of the Nile River but died in 1873 before achieving his goal. Stanley later returned to Africa and explored Lake Victoria. He confirmed that the Kagera River and its tributaries, which fed Lake Victoria, were the source of the Nile River.

Modern Cities, Ancient Roots

Today, more than seven million people live in Egypt's crowded capital, Cairo. The city has many office buildings, universities, factories, and homes. Yet, the people of Cairo are constantly reminded of the distant past. For more than 1,000 years, the city has stood on the same site. Ancient royal palaces have been turned into modern hotels.

A 3,000-year-old temple is located in the middle of the modern city of Luxor. This was also the site of the ancient Egyptian city of Thebes. Today, more than 400,000 people live there.

People paddle on the Sobat River, a tributary of the White Nile, near the town of Nassir in southern Sudan.

The economy of Luxor is based mostly on tourism. Large numbers of people also farm sugarcane.

Aswan, Egypt, stands on the ruins of the ancient city of Yeb. Today, Aswan is a commercial and industrial center. Factories there produce fertilizer and cement, and **quarries** yield granite and marble. The same quarries supplied granite for many ancient Egyptian monuments.

Village People

The Nile River also passes through many small, quiet villages. A wide variety of people live along the great river. **Bantu**-speaking people live in the area around Lake Victoria. Bantu is a group of languages spoken in central and southern Africa.

The Dinka and the Nuer are the two largest ethnic groups in southern Sudan. The Dinka are herders who move with the Nile River's seasonal flow. During the dry season, they stay close to the river's shores. During the wet season, they move to higher ground. The Nuer live in the western region of southern Sudan. The two groups often compete for land.

CHAPTER 4

Travel and Commerce

The Nile River has been a major transportation route in Egypt since ancient times. The Nile River helped the people in the region stay connected. It also enabled them to transport and trade goods, such as grain, spices, and livestock. This "water highway" was an important element in the development of a unified civilization.

Traveling the Nile

Ancient Egyptians used boats of different sizes to travel to towns along the Nile River. The size and type of boat depended on the part of the Nile River being traveled. People traveling south used flat-bottomed boats and put up sails. These ancient sailboats were called feluccas. The wind helped move the boats over the water. To return home to the north, Egyptians took down the sails and drifted with the natural flow of the river.

Rough Waters

Cataracts and white-water **gorges** characterize parts of the Nile River's course. In these areas, large wooden boats would have been destroyed. People did not use large freighters or passenger ships on these waters. They used small, canoe-like boats and fishing boats. People could **portage**, or carry, these boats around cataracts and rapids.

Damming the Flow

In the 1860s, British engineers began building small dams across the Nile River. Dams made travel easier because

FAST FACT

Ancient Egyptians used cedar trees imported from Lebanon to build some of their boats. Lebanon is on the eastern shore of the Mediterranean Sea.

they controlled the flow of water. Dams also captured some of the annual floodwaters for irrigation during the dry months.

In the early 1900s, a large dam was built near the city of Aswan. Called the Aswan Dam, it provided irrigation but could not completely contain the flooding. In 1971, another, larger dam—the Aswan High Dam—was completed. The construction of the Aswan High Dam changed life in Egypt forever. This dam and others strengthened Egypt's agricultural economy, since crops could now be

LEFT: A traditional felucca boat sails on the Nile River at Aswan.

The Aswan High Dam captures Nile River floodwater, which is stored in a reservoir and released during dry periods. The dam also uses the Nile River's water to generate enormous amounts of electricity.

irrigated all year long. The economic benefits of the Aswan High Dam have enabled the government to build more schools, hospitals, and modern sewage systems.

The Aswan High Dam is also a source of hydroelectric power. Power from the dam provides electricity for Cairo and several other large Egyptian cities. Electricity from the dam powers big factories as well.

Tourist Attraction

There was also a large increase in tourism after the Aswan High Dam was completed and the man-made Lake Nasser was created. Tourism has contributed greatly to Egypt's economy. Millions of visitors take boating and fishing trips and stop at ancient Egyptian temples and pyramids along the Nile. Some people tour the river on traditional feluccas. Tours can last a few hours, several days, or several weeks.

Birth of a Lake

The Aswan High Dam created a huge reservoir known as Lake Nasser. The lake soon became a tourist attraction and a recreational area. The creation of Lake Nasser had many negative effects, too. For example, ancient temples and monuments were flooded. The temple of Abu Simbel, built by Ramses II, took four years and cost $40 million to save. It had to be cut into more than 1,000 blocks and put back together on higher land.

From 1966 to 1968, work crews carved the great temple of Abu Simbel into pieces. The temple was reassembled on an artificial hill above Lake Nasser.

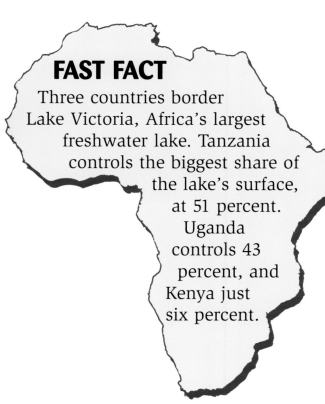

FAST FACT

Three countries border Lake Victoria, Africa's largest freshwater lake. Tanzania controls the biggest share of the lake's surface, at 51 percent. Uganda controls 43 percent, and Kenya just six percent.

Tourists also travel to the Nile River to see the Tisisat Falls on the Blue Nile in Ethiopia. Millions of gallons of water drop over the cliff face into a gorge. Tourists may even see spectacular rainbows as the water drops.

Lake Victoria is another popular tourist destination. It is the second-largest freshwater lake in the world. Lake Victoria is widely used for transportation and recreation. Its shoreline is more than 2,000 miles (3,220 km) long. It has more than 3,000 islands, and most of them are inhabited. The Sese Islands, in the northwest part of the lake, are a popular tourist destination.

CHAPTER 5

The Nile River Today

Today, giant dams on the Nile River generate electricity for almost half the people living along the river. Billions of gallons of water come from modern irrigation pumps, so farmers can grow grains, vegetables, and fruit year-round. Water from the Nile River also flows through the plumbing of modern skyscrapers, apartments, and houses in cities. But the actions of humans have also harmed the river and the land around it in lasting ways.

Troubled Waters

For thousands of years, the annual Nile River floods brought tons of silt to the riverbanks and delta. The fertility of the land along the Nile River depended greatly on the rich deposits of the floodwaters. Today, dams prevent the Nile River from flooding, so silt can no longer reach crops. As a result, the farmland surrounding the Nile River is not as fertile, and the food crops are not as plentiful. Many farmers now must use chemical fertilizers on their crops. The chemicals can be dangerous for the animals and people that ingest them, or take them in.

Some experts say that without the yearly deposit of sediment, the river delta has been eroding, or wearing away. The Aswan High Dam has also reduced the flow of the river, allowing saltwater from the Mediterranean Sea to force its way up the Nile River. An increase in the amount of salt in soil and irrigation water harms farm crops. Valuable farmland in the delta is gradually disappearing.

LEFT: Cairo is the capital of Egypt and is the most populous city in Africa.

People have also introduced **invasive species** to the Nile River system, both intentionally, as decorative plants, for example, and unintentionally on ships. These nonnative species take over the habitats of the plants and animals that are indigenous to the area. Invasive species can crowd out or prey on native river species, causing them to die out.

Poverty and Pollution

The countries along the Upper Nile— Rwanda, Burundi, Tanzania, and Uganda—are some of the poorest countries in the world. The populations of these countries

Factories in industrial areas along the Nile River discharge materials that pollute the river.

Water Woes

Politics affected by water and water resources is sometimes called **hydropolitics**. The Nile River passes through several countries, and people in those countries have different ideas about how the river should be used. In recent years, disputes have occurred over water rights and changes to the river's natural flow.

continue to grow. Many new towns and villages do not have modern sanitation, and people dump tons of garbage and human waste into the Nile River. As a result, people, plants, and animals are being poisoned by contaminated drinking water. The thousands of small factories in these countries are not yet **regulated**. They dump all kinds of wastes directly into the Nile River.

FAST FACT

Climate change is causing sea levels around the world to rise. Some scientists predict that coastal areas along the Nile River delta could be flooded by the end of the century.

Population Growth

During the 20th century, the populations along the Nile River increased dramatically. At the beginning of the 19th century, the population of Egypt was 4.3 million. Today, the population is 65 million. People constantly need more water from the Nile River for drinking, washing, and industrial use. As a result, the Nile River is being polluted. Too little water is available to meet the needs of people in all the countries along the river's course. Many scientists who study the Nile River believe that population growth must be slowed. If it cannot be slowed, the Nile River may not be able to support life as it has for thousands of years.

Seeking Solutions

Scientists, engineers, politicians, environmentalists, and others are working to solve some of the Nile's problems. Some engineers believe that improving the design of dams would help resolve some concerns. They say

A sprinkler system, such as the one watering this field of potatoes, is more efficient than earlier irrigation methods.

small earthen dams, called check dams, are good alternatives to giant structures like the Aswan High Dam. Check dams allow silt to flow to fields, keeping the soil nourished. Small dams are unable to generate electricity, however.

New irrigation systems may also bring improvements. Long, open irrigation ditches are being replaced with sprinkler irrigation systems. Sprinkler systems use less water and provide better water control because they pump water evenly. Farmers are also beginning to use drip irrigation systems for watering tree and vine crops, such as dates, figs, grapes, and olives. Drip irrigation is less expensive than sprinkler systems.

The Nile Basin Initiative

In 1999, the Nile Basin Initiative was established. It is a partnership among ten countries along the Nile River, including Eritrea, which shares only a very small portion of the Nile River basin. A committee reviews proposed projects for the Nile River and works to protect the river basin.

COMPARING THE WORLD'S RIVERS

River	Continent	Source	Outflow	Approximate Length in miles (kilometers)	Area of Drainage Basin in square miles (square kilometers)
Amazon	South America	Andes Mountains, Peru	Atlantic Ocean	4,000 (6,450)	2.7 million (7 million)
Euphrates	Asia	Murat and Kara Su rivers, Turkey	Persian Gulf	1,740 (2,800)	171,430 (444,000)
Ganges	Asia	Himalayas, India	Bay of Bengal	1,560 (2,510)	400,000 (1 million)
Mississippi	North America	Lake Itasca, Minnesota	Gulf of Mexico	2,350 (3,780)	1.2 million (3.1 million)
Nile	Africa	Streams flowing into Lake Victoria, East Africa	Mediterranean Sea	4,145 (6,670)	1.3 million (3.3 million)
Rhine	Europe	Alps, Switzerland	North Sea	865 (1,390)	65,600 (170,000)
St. Lawrence	North America	Lake Ontario, Canada and United States	Gulf of St. Lawrence	744 (1,190)	502,000 (1.3 million)
Tigris	Asia	Lake Hazar, Taurus Mountains, Turkey	Persian Gulf	1,180 (1,900)	43,000 (111,000)
Yangtze	Asia	Damqu River, Tanggula Mountains, China	East China Sea	3,915 (6,300)	690,000 (1.8 million)

TIMELINE

About 30 million years ago	The Nile River begins to form.
4000–1500 BC	The Sahara Desert forms.
3400 BC	An ancient Egyptian civilization begins to develop.
3100 BC	The Egyptian empire is formed from the kingdoms along the Nile River.
3000 BC	Papyrus writing material is developed.
About 450 BC	Greek historian Herodotus travels to Egypt.
66 AD	Roman explorers set sail up the Nile River to find its source but stop at the Sudd.
969	The city of Cairo is first settled at its present-day location.
1770	Scottish explorer James Bruce reaches Lake Tana, the source of the Blue Nile.
1858	John Hanning Speke reaches Lake Victoria.
1861	Engineers complete the first modern irrigation system in the Nile River delta.
1902	British engineers complete the first phase of the Aswan Dam, near the city of Aswan, Egypt.
1970	The Aswan High Dam is completed, ending the annual flooding of the Nile River in Egypt.
1999	The Nile Basin Initiative is established by nations sharing the Nile River basin, in an effort to protect the river basin from environmental damage.

GLOSSARY

Bantu A group of African languages

carnivore An animal that eats meat

cataracts Large waterfalls

delta A triangular or fan-shaped area of land at the mouth of a river

dendritic Branching like a tree

drainage basin The area of land drained by a river and its tributaries

drainage pattern The arrangement of a main stream and its tributaries

ecology The relationship between living and nonliving things and their environment

economy The way money and goods are produced, consumed, and distributed

geologists Scientists who study the history of Earth and its life, especially as recorded in rocks

glaciers Large bodies of ice and snow moving slowly down a slope or spreading outward on land

gorges Narrow canyons with steep walls

groundwater Water within Earth, especially that supplies wells and springs

habitat The environment in which a plant or an animal naturally lives and grows

headstream A stream that forms the source of a river

hydroelectricity Electricity that is produced by the movement of water

hydropolitics Conflict and cooperation between governments with respect to water resources

indigenous Originating, living, or occurring naturally in a particular region or environment

inundation: Overflow of floodwaters

invasive species Species that do not naturally occur in a specific area and that cause economic or environmental harm to that area

irrigation The watering of land in an artificial way to foster plant growth

migratory Moving periodically from one region or climate to another for feeding or breeding

mouth The place where a river enters a larger body of water

mummy A dead body treated for burial with preservatives in the manner of the ancient Egyptians

papyrus A reed-like plant that can be made into strips and pressed into a material to write on

pharaohs Rulers of ancient Egypt

portage To carry boats or goods overland from one body of water to another or around an obstacle (such as rapids)

predator An animal that gets its food by hunting and eating other animals

quarries Open pits, usually for obtaining building stone

regulated Controlled by law or another authority

reservoirs Artificial lakes in which water is collected and kept for use

rifts Cracks in Earth's crust that widen over time

runoff Water from rain or snow that flows over the surface of the ground and into rivers

silt Small particles of sand or rock left as sediment

tributaries Smaller rivers and streams that flow into larger bodies of water

FIND OUT MORE

BOOKS

Bowden, Rob. *Settlements of the River Nile*. Heinemann-Raintree, 2005.

Ylvisaker, Anne. *The Nile River*. Compass Point Books, 2005.

Challen, Paul. *Life in Ancient Egypt*. Crabtre Publishing Company, 2005

Ylvisaker, Anne. *The Nile River*. Compass Point Books, 2005.

Moscovitch, Arlene. *Egypt the Land. (Revised edition)*.
    Crabtree Publishing Company, 2008

WEB SITES

International Rivers: About Rivers
www.internationalrivers.org/en/node/288

KidsPast.com: The Nile Valley
www.kidspast.com/world-history/0029-nile-river-valley.php

National Geographic: Ethiopia's Sacred Waters—The Blue Nile
http//ngm.nationalgeographic.com/ngm/0012/feature1/index.html

ABOUT THE AUTHOR

Molly Aloian has written more than 50 nonfiction books for children on a wide variety of topics, including endangered animals, animal life cycles, continents and their geography, holidays around the world, and chemistry. When she is not busy writing, she enjoys traveling, hiking, and cooking.

INDEX

Page references in **bold** type are to illustrations.